WELCOME TO
DEATH VALLEY
NATIONAL PARK

BY M.J. COSSON

Many thanks to the staff at Death Valley National Park for their assistance with this book.

MAP KEY

The maps throughout this
book use the following icons:

 Driving Excursion

 Hiking Trail

 Campground

 Information Center

 Overlook

 Point of Interest

 Ranger Station

 Visitor Center

 Wildflower Area

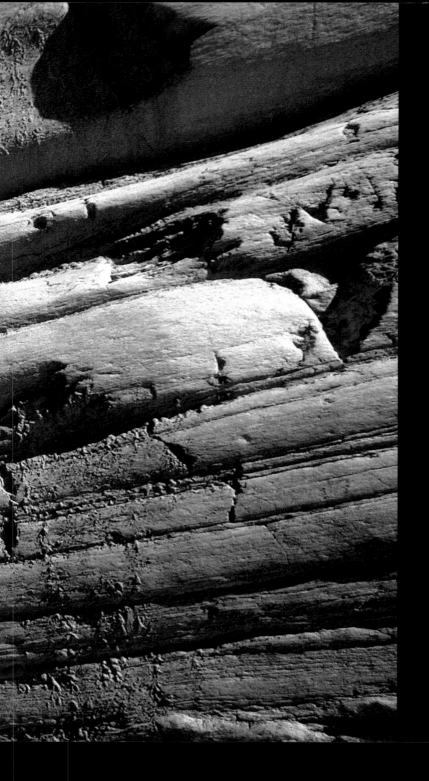

About National Parks

A national park is an area of land that has been set aside by Congress. National parks protect nature and history. In most cases, no hunting, grazing, or farming is allowed. The first national park in the United States—and in the world—was Yellowstone National Park. It is located in parts of Wyoming, Idaho, and Montana. It was founded in 1872. In 1916, the U.S. National Park Service began.

Today, the National Park Service manages more than 380 sites. Some of these sites are historic, such as the Statue of Liberty or Martin Luther King, Jr. National Historic Site. Other park areas preserve wild land. The National Park Service manages 40% of the nation's wilderness areas, including national parks. Each year, millions of people from around the world visit these national parks. Visitors may camp, go canoeing, or go for a hike. Or, they may simply sit and enjoy the scenery, wildlife, and the quiet of the land.

TABLE OF

The Child's World®

Published in the United States of America by The Child's World®

PO Box 326
Chanhassen, MN 55317-0326
800-599-READ
www.childsworld.com

Acknowledgements
The Child's World®: Mary Berendes, Publishing Director

Content Consultant: Nancy Hadlock, Park Ranger, Interpretation, Death Valley National Park

The Design Lab: Kathleen Petelinsek, Design and Page Production

Map Hero, Inc.: Matt Kania, Cartographer

Red Line Editorial: Bob Temple, Editorial Direction

Photo Credits
Cover and this page: Bob Krist/Corbis

Interior: Bob Krist/ Corbis: 15; BrandXPictures: 1, 2-3, 6-7, 19, 23; Carl & Ann Purcell/ Corbis: 26; Corbis: 13; Darrell Gulin/ Corbis: 8; Dave G. Houser/Post-Houserstock/ Corbis: 20–21; George H. H. Huey/ Corbis: 24–25 ; Gordon Whitten/ Corbis: 12; Hans Strand/ Corbis: 9; J. Emilio Flores/ Corbis: 11; Phil Schermeister/ Corbis: 16; Terry W. Eggers/ Corbis: 22

Library of Congress Cataloging-in-Publication Data
Cosson, M. J.
   Welcome to Death Valley National Park / by M.J. Cosson.
       p. cm. — (Visitor guides)
   Includes index.
   ISBN 1-59296-694-2 (library bound : alk. paper)
   1. Death Valley National Park (Calif. and Nev.)—Juvenile literature. I. Title. II. Series.
   F868.D2C78 2006
   917.94'870454—dc22   2005030078

On the cover and this page
Joshua trees grow in many areas of Death Valley National Park. They are named for their upturned branches, which reminded long-ago settlers of Joshua, a man from the Bible who often raised his arms in prayer.

On page 1
In some areas of the park, the landscape changes quickly from wind-sculpted sand dunes to jagged mountains.

On pages 2–3
Mosaic Canyon is just one of the park's beautiful sights. The canyon's marble walls were carved by water over thousands of years.

WELCOME TO DEATH VALLEY NATIONAL PARK

∧

CONTENTS

Can Things Live Here?

CALIFORNIA

Death Valley National Park

Welcome to Death Valley National Park! Death Valley is known for its strange yet beautiful landscapes. It is the second largest national park—and the largest national park in the lower 48 states. Death Valley is also the lowest, driest, and hottest place in the country. In summer, it's best to visit in an air-conditioned car. You can park and take short hikes. Be sure to bring water, sunscreen, and a hat. The temperature could be as high as 125 degrees F (52 C)!

The Shoshone people have lived here for a very long time. The Shoshone moved to the mountains during summer. Other Native American people lived here as long as 14,000 years ago. Miners have lived here, too. If people stayed through the summer, they were at risk of death. You might think that nothing can possibly live in this desert. However, many different plants and animals live here. They have **adapted** to in Death Valley.

The wind shapes the park's sand dunes into waves and creases in many areas. The wind is only able to shape the sand if there is little to no water keeping the grains together—so the park's dry weather is perfect for sand shaping!

🚶🚶 A coyote takes an afternoon nap in the rocks near Furnace Creek. Coyotes are active mostly at night, but will also hunt for food during the daytime—especially if they have babies to feed.

You'll notice that the air is very clear in Death Valley. Everything looks crisp, and the sky is deep blue. You don't hear many noises. You won't see many animals during the day. One way animals have adapted to life in Death Valley is to be **nocturnal**. This means they are active at night when it's cooler.

The Desert Valley

Death Valley is a mix of **geologic** features. Cracks, or faults, in Earth's crust caused mountains to rise and the valley to sink. Volcanoes formed some of the mountains and added to the colorful rocks. Weather and gravity have played a part, too. All of these forces are still shaping Death Valley today.

Mountain Blockade

Air currents gather moisture from the ocean. The moist air blows onto land. It rises when it hits mountains. As the air rises, it cools and forms clouds. Rain and snow fall mostly on the ocean side of the mountains. The mountains block moisture from Death Valley, which helps to keep it a desert.

Blooming Color

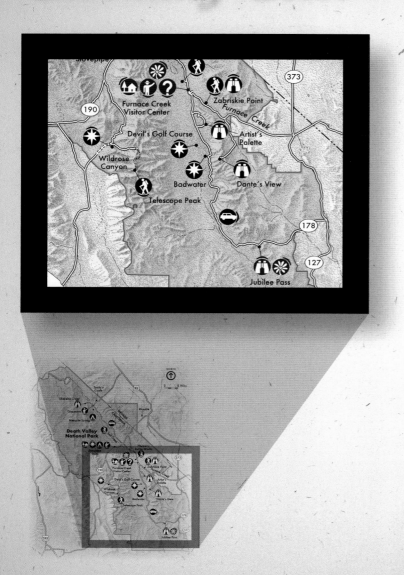

Watch for colorful wildflowers, especially near Furnace Creek Inn or Jubilee Pass. Wildflower seeds have thick or waxy coats. The seeds can stay **dormant** for years. Death Valley usually receives less than 2 inches (5 cm) of rainfall each year. In a year with heavy rainfall, the wildflower seeds come alive. You can see desert star, blazing star, and desert lupine. Only in Death Valley can you see Eureka Dunes evening primrose, Death Valley monkeyflower, and the bright yellow Panamint daisy.

The cacti are blooming, too. Look for cottontop barrel, silver cholla, beavertail, and grizzly-bear prickly pear. Because Death Valley is so salty, you might see more creosote or saltbush plants than cactus.

Desert sunflowers are very common throughout the park. These golden wildflowers grow to be about 3 feet (1 m) high, and their seeds are an important food for birds and mice.

Views like these are common in Death Valley: low bushes and grasses that grow apart from each other. Here you can see a field of salt-loving plants that grow well in very dry, salty soil.

Some plants have deep roots that seek water in cracks of the rocks. The creosote bush has a wide, shallow root system. The roots produce a poison to keep other bushes from growing nearby. That way, other plants won't take the creosote's water.

Look down into Death Valley and you might not see any plants. That's because it is so low and salty. Look up to the mountains and you will see piñon pine and juniper trees.

Desert Food Chain

The wildflowers begin a desert food chain. Big, fat caterpillars that develop into Sphinx moths eat the flowers. Birds and small **rodents** make a meal of the caterpillars and moths. Snakes and foxes hunt the birds and rodents.

From Good Water to Badwater

S top at the Furnace Creek Visitor Center and Museum. Look at the exhibits and the slide program. Find out about the walks that are available and the nature programs. Stop to watch a roadrunner dart away. This bird is a member of the cuckoo family. It tends to run instead of flying.

The springs at Furnace Creek produce more than 1 million gallons (3.8 million liters) of fresh water each day. This makes the Furnace Creek area an **oasis** in the desert. Near Furnace Creek, look for oleanders, palm trees, tamarask trees, and even a golf course!

🚶🚶 The Furnace Creek Golf Course is a popular place with golfers. A rancher started the course in 1925 by building a tiny, three-hole course on the site. Another six holes were added in the 1950s, and it became a full 18-hole course by the 1960s. Golfers here must be careful, however, as daytime temperatures often reach 115 F (46 C).

The lake that once covered Devil's Golf Course was only about 600 feet (183 m) deep. When the lake dried up, it left a layer of salty mud about 3 to 5 feet (1 to 1.5 m) thick. Over the years, the wind and rain shaped the salty mud into countless lumps and hills—making the area a place where "only the Devil could play golf."

Your next stop is Devil's Golf Course. It is not like the golf course at Furnace Creek. Two thousand years ago, there was a lake in Death Valley. The rock-salt crystals formed when the shallow, salty lake dried up. The crystals continue to form and change as wind and rain hit them. Listen carefully. You might hear a "pop" and "ping" as they change!

When you reach Badwater, you will be standing in the lowest place in North America. It dips 282 feet (86 m) below sea level! You might wonder how Badwater got its name. The water at Badwater Springs is much too salty to drink. It is several times saltier than the ocean.

Colors and Contrasts

Take a side trip through Artist's Palette on your way north. See the rainbow of colors in the rocks. Different **minerals** make each color, and Death Valley is rich in minerals.

Head further north to Zabriskie Point. From here you can look down into the badlands. Notice how the wind and rain have shaped the clay mud. Few plants grow here. You can walk the canyon to get a closer view.

Next, take the trail to the Harmony Borax Works. **Borax** was mined in Death Valley from 1883 to 1888. During the California gold rush, **prospectors** came looking for gold. They found gold, along with silver, lead, tungsten, copper, borax, and talc. Today, the U.S. government protects Death Valley's mines and minerals.

Death Valley's landscape is breathtaking, especially at sunset. The colors of the rocks and hills seem to change as the sun rises and sets every day.

Salt Creek flows south into Death Valley. It is only about 3 inches (7.5 cm) deep in most areas. Plants such as salt grass, saltbush, and pickleweed often grow in or near the creek, which provides protection and shade for the pupfish.

Mule Teams

In the 1880s, mule teams hauled borax out of Death Valley to the railroad 165 miles (266 km) away. Each team of 18 mules and two horses pulled two wagons and a water tank that weighed 36.5 tons altogether. They began 190 feet (58 m) below sea level and climbed to 2,000 feet (610 m) above sea level. What a tough climb!

Salt Creek is as salty as the ocean. Walk along the boardwalk to see small Salt Creek pupfish. When the lake in Death Valley **evaporated**, small amounts of salty water remained. Salt Creek pupfish adapted to the new **environment**. Many die during summer, when most of the water evaporates. During winter they burrow into the mud. When the spring rains come, they're swimming again. Pupfish live mostly in North American deserts.

Nighttime in Death Valley

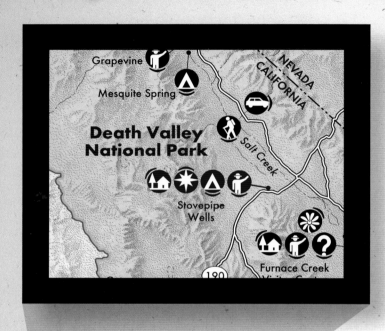

At last, you reach the sand dunes near Stovepipe Wells. The sand here is made of tiny grains of quartz. The wind has blown the grains into wave shapes. You can run up and down the waves of sand. You can look for animal tracks in the sand. You can watch the dunes turn a rosy pink, from the setting sun.

Stay at Stovepipe Wells overnight. You can camp or stay in a motel. Before you turn in, look for bats darting through the air. Dusk brings cottontail rabbits, jackrabbits, kangaroo rats, flycatchers, and scorpions. You might also see a kit fox or a pocket mouse.

The sand dunes near Stovepipe Wells are some of the most photographed in the world. During the day, the dunes' colors and shapes often look flat and boring. But at sunrise, sunset, or even in the moonlight, the wavy dunes become a spectacular sight.

You might even see a sidewinder moving across the sand. It's easy to tell how this rattlesnake got its name. Like many desert animals, the sidewinder doesn't drink water. It gets its moisture from the animals it eats.

Listen! A coyote is crying at the moon. Now look up. Bats have replaced the flycatchers swooping through the sky.

Somewhere in Death Valley, the desert's biggest mammals roam. The desert bighorn sheep and the mule deer are mostly in mountain areas. The bobcat and the mountain lion are nearby as well, hunting for a good meal.

and largest of a number of craters and volcanic features in the area. The crater is an awesome sight, being more than a

In the morning you can continue north to Ubehebe Crater. You will see a volcano. When the hot **magma** from underground met the groundwater several thousand years ago, it caused an explosion. You may think you're looking at the moon!

Ninety-five percent of Death Valley is wilderness. You have only explored a small bit of the park. There are many trails you can take and many more sights to see. Death Valley is a land of great beauty and contrasts, but its summer heat can be dangerous. Come and explore all that Death Valley has to offer, but make sure that you come prepared to keep yourself safe from the elements.

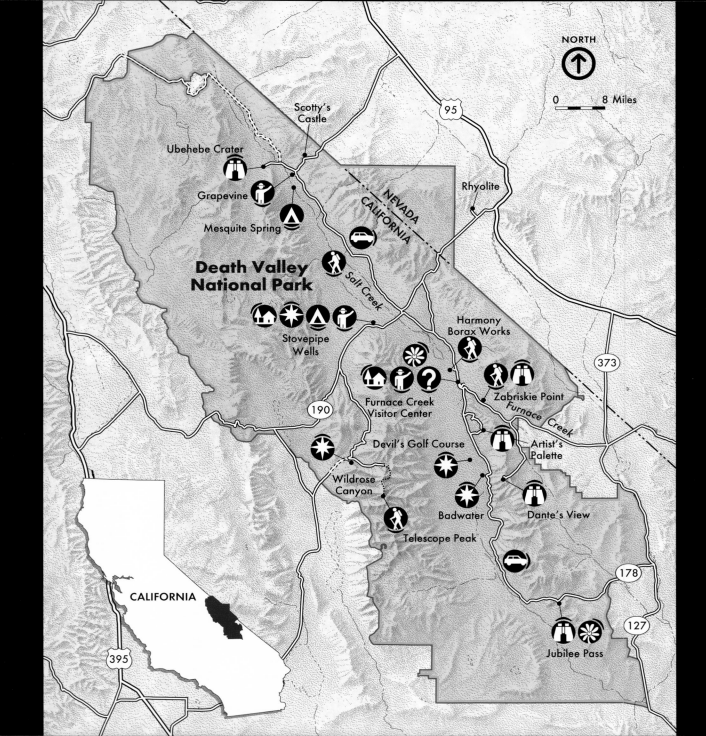

NORTH

0   8 Miles

95

Scotty's Castle

Ubehebe Crater

Grapevine

Mesquite Spring

Rhyolite

NEVADA
CALIFORNIA

Death Valley National Park

Salt Creek

Stovepipe Wells

Harmony Borax Works

Furnace Creek Visitor Center

Zabriskie Point

Furnace Creek

373

Devil's Golf Course

Artist's Palette

Wildrose Canyon

Badwater

Dante's View

Telescope Peak

178

127

CALIFORNIA

Jubilee Pass

395

190

28

DEATH VALLEY NATIONAL PARK FAST FACTS

Date opened: February 11, 1933 as a national monument; October 31, 1994 as a national park

Location: Eastern California and a small area of western Nevada

Size: 5,269 square miles/13,647 sq km; 3.4 million acres/1.4 million hectares

Major habitat: Desert—part of Mojave (south) and Great Basin (north) desert ecosystems

Elevation:
   Highest: 11,049 feet/3,368 m (Telescope Peak in the Panamint Mountains)
   Lowest: 282 feet/86 m below sea level (Badwater)

Weather:
   Average yearly rainfall: Less than 2 inches/5 cm
   Average temperatures (Furnace Creek area):
   106 F/41 C to 48 F/9 C
   Highest temperature: 134 F/57 C (1913)

Number of animal species: 346 kinds of birds, 36 reptile species, 5 amphibian species, 5 fish species, and 51 types of mammals

Number of plant species: 1,042, including about 23 that are found only in Death Valley

Native people: Shoshone

Number of visitors each year: About 1.3 million

Important sites and landmarks: Scotty's Castle, ghost towns such as Rhyolite at the east edge (outside the park), Natural Bridge Canyon, Wildrose Canyon charcoal kilns, Mosaic Canyon, Dante's View, Funeral Mountains, Borax Museum and Harmony Borax Works, the Racetrack (Death Valley's playa, where strong winds make rocks skid across the mud surface), Lost Burro Mine, and Titus Canyon

Tourist activities: Hiking, bird watching, nature walks and talks, geology classes, horseback riding, bicycling, and camping

GLOSSARY

adapted (uh-DAP-ted): When something has changed to fit in its environment, it has adapted. The Salt Creek pupfish adapted to life in Death Valley.

borax (BOR-ax): Borax is a white solid that occurs in salty soils. Borax is used to clean things and to make glass.

dormant (DORM-unt): Things that are not active and not growing or changing are dormant. Wildflower seeds can lay dormant for many years.

environment (en-VY-run-ment): All of the things in an area are called the environment. Death Valley can be a very harsh environment.

evaporated (eh-VAP-uh-rayt-ed): When a liquid has changed into a gas, it has evaporated. Water can evaporate quickly in the hot desert.

geologic (jee-uh-LOJ-ik): Geologic things have to do with the rocks and minerals of Earth or another planet. Death Valley is a good place for geologic studies.

magma (MAG-muh): Magma is liquid rock. Volcanoes shot magma that makes some of the beautiful colors in Death Valley.

minerals (MIN-er-ullz): Nonliving materials found in rocks and dirt are minerals. Borax and gold are two minerals that have been found in Death Valley.

nocturnal (nok-TURN-ull): Animals that are active at night are nocturnal. Bats and sidewinders are nocturnal.

oasis (oh-AY-sis): A place in a desert where fresh water makes plants grow is called an oasis. Furnace Creek springs from an oasis in Death Valley.

prospectors (PRAH-spek-turz): A prospector is someone who explores to find gold, silver, or other minerals. Prospectors searched Death Valley for minerals.

rodents (ROH-dents): Small mammals such as mice or squirrels with teeth that keep growing all their lives are called rodents. Kangaroo rats are rodents.

TO FIND OUT MORE

FURTHER READING

Cooper, Jason.
Death Valley.
Vero Beach, FL: Rourke, 1995.

Duey, Kathleen and Karen A. Bale.
Survival! Death Valley (California 1849).
New York: Aladdin, 1998.

Petersen, David.
Death Valley National Park.
New York: Children's Press, 1996.

ON THE WEB

Visit our home page for lots of links about
Death Valley National Park:

http://www.childsworld.com/links

NOTE TO PARENTS, TEACHERS, AND LIBRARIANS:
We routinely check our Web links to make sure
they're safe, active sites—so encourage your
readers to check them out!

🏃🏃 **ABOUT THE AUTHOR**
M.J. Cosson has written
many books for children. She
lives in the Texas Hill Country.
She has also lived in the desert
of New Mexico. She thinks
the desert is beautiful and its
animals are some of the most
amazing on Earth.

INDEX